GUMBO YA YA

PITT POETRY SERIES

ED OCHESTER, EDITOR

GUMBO YA YA

AURIELLE MARIE

UNIVERSITY OF PITTSBURGH PRESS

THIS BOOK IS THE WINNER OF THE 2020 CAVE CANEM POETRY PRIZE, SELECTED BY DOUGLAS KEARNEY

Founded in 1996 by poets Toi Derricotte and Cornelius Eady, Cave Canem is a home for the many voices of African American poetry and is committed to cultivating the artistic and professional growth of African American poets.

Established in 1999, the Cave Canem Poetry Prize is awarded annually to an exceptional manuscript by an African American poet who has not yet published a full-length book of poems.

Support for the Cave Canem Poetry Prize has been provided, in part, from The Ford Foundation, Lannan Foundation, and individual donors.

Published by the University of Pittsburgh Press, Pittsburgh, Pa., 15260

Manufactured in the United States of America
Printed on acid-free paper
10 9 8 7 6 5 4 3 2 1

ISBN 13: 978-0-8229-6666-1
ISBN 10: 0-8229-6666-2

COVER ART: Tschabalala Self, *Nate the Snake*, 2020. Digital print on canvas, fabric, thread, stamped canvas, painted canvas, dyed canvas, acrylic and hand mixed pigments on canvas, 213½ × 152½ × 4 cm / 84 × 60 × 1½ in. © Tschabalala Self. Marieluise Hessel Collection, Hessel Museum of Art, Center for Curatorial Studies, Bard College, Annandale-on-Hudson, New York. Photo by Matt Grubb.

COVER DESIGN: Alex Wolfe

For me.
For mama, and my sister-cousins.
For my egun.
For all the grxls that have
built safe places for me—
in their arms,
on their chests, by their faith—
Thank you. I carry you.

I can tell you that from now on my resistance
my simple daily and nightly self-determination
may very well cost you your life

• JUNE JORDAN •

CONTENTS

gum·bo ya·ya 🔊 n.

(/ˈgəmbō/ \ yäˈyä \) · Creole-English origin.

1. A wild-making noise from the mouths of loved ones, particularly in great joy or grief, so loud and unabashed that it overwhelms the senses.
2. A too-loud thing that cannot be contained by a room
3. The soup of noise made by everyone talking at once, so much so, that
 a. an entirely new, distinct sound is made
 b. the noise-makers are themselves made new by the loud, untamed uproar of their own creation
4. A fine clayey soil that becomes sticky and impervious when wet, most notably under the nails of Black femmes.

[alternate spellings: **gumbo yah·yah, gum·bo, gum·beaux, black gxrl**]

v. (/ˈgəmbō/ \ yäˈyä \)

1. Noise
 a. To create from nothing
  b. To survive at an intersection
   c. And fight to be made visible

notes & acknowledgments

well, first I want to recognize the land
we stand on is stolen

let it be said here, at least
that all Black lives matter
that water is indeed life
& above all things

we the people is
how any patriot
begins his lie.

I acknowledge the author
tried to craft a project with siloed agendas
pursued poems as small acts of war
or love letters for a father,
daggers for the 45th president but
those invocations must wait.

I write to you with a soft
hand and gritted teeth
I acknowledge the rhetorical
struggles, myths, and obligations
I acknowledge we are not allowed
any singular monuments.

understand, reader
the world is seldom mine
to build; but is indeed, here, ours.
thick with odes & laments. ours &
built by the blood of ebonix, atomized
libraries and anything coaxing our
pleasures erect

Black gxrls—or, as the evening
news has named us, extremists—
are kindred in this anti-making,
already cooking feasts out the dried
skin of nationalists. feasts with our jewels
and old mothers. feasts, sankofa & broth.
we rid this world of all its guns
and elbows, its gum and marrow.

i slurry out a poem from th new world,
stir it into a meal and its name is *yaya*—wild.
welcome. this new world, hallowed by swarms of bees
and languages chewed outta jazz.

ours, this world, enraged
by even a splinter interrupting
the palm of our wildest gxrls

I acknowledge

I acknowledge

I am angry. I am tired. I am scared. I am lonely. I am angry. I am angry. I am. I am.
You will hear what you want. I will be what you make of me.

I am angry.
I am angry.
I am angry.
I am angry.
I am angry.
I am angry.
I am angry.
I am angry.
I am angry.
I am angry.
I am angry.
I am angry.
I am angry.
I am angry.
I am angry.
I am angry

/ / /

I admit: the author's hands are broken,
hashtags holding open our mouths. hands
like a *no* world, made yes. made magical &
with child. with poems & a new gospel, we be-
gin folding starshine & clay into small trumpets
—listen

blood flammable | knuckle soured
intoxicated by blues | our hands
like vowels | verbs | alive & billowed
little fathers | our hands | wild cotton
choir-holy | if we die | use ambulance siren
for our names

/ / /

I intend to steal
from you, your comfort   I intend to steal I intend to steal stealsteal
I intend to steal
I intend to steal I intend to steal
& gift it to a Black gxrl   I intend to steal
I intend to steal
who broke her hot comb on **I intend to steal** I intend to steal
I intend to steal
the morning's rough edge   I intend **I intend to steal** I intend to

/ / /

there are, these worlds
to labor toward, too:

1) in which none of the Black gxrls die
1) in which death is only a doorway
1) in which the series *Girlfriends* never dies like us it goes on
1) in which i call for my gxrlfriends and mean

[from the barrel of the law]
[crying *fire* instead of rape]
[for loving an other Black grxl]
[during childbirth]
& the egun
forever
lover or maybe *mother*.
doula. *muse*. *survivor*, or
god.

/ / /

aight reader, let's keep it
a buck: i will lie to you.
let it be for your good.

the truths under which we survive
have begun to splinter: children
spilling blood instead of marigolds
from their hands, the mad kings
snorting our money like pollen
and now even cicadas lie silent as the ballots are counted.

reader, you gotta admit, *this world been failin*
us. sometimes i will too. i bring no remedy.
i'm afraid & i only know what i do not know.

i acknowledge death but don't
truly believe i am afforded
object permeance or linear
time. i am absolute & unresolved
no matter how the poem dresses it up.

i acknowledge this
as a joint contract.
you will do with it
what you must.

[yes, you must
do somethin.
if not, then what is
the point?]

what had happened
(a nigga analysis on applied rhetorics)

clock the first/young
break, english like ugly
time/bully or
counter/tongue

had happened/yet to happen,
it was happening/already over
the verte/

break/time like
belligerent maths, do what a
scythe can to a nigga/neck

this land
shole nuff had happened/been
born inordinate/swole with
the language of it's
stolen/employee

what was indeed/broken
was simple/considering all possibilities
and their trans/linear
contrary/proportions

had a collection
happened of almosts

before a boat *had*
a place happened into Georgia
culled then by dissimilar/sound
knowing it could not be named
before it became,
it became

and language is only the thing/fractured
by an hour/circle of iron
around a nigga/neck

been did
tryna be
finna and
any/other
whole account of history

what must/transpire
between a crop/blooming sand/into sugar

what had happened/balm upon the entire testimony:

I lost/ my mouth/ & grew/ an hourglass

gxrl gospel i: all the women were white, all of the Black folk, men & so, we were brave

"and it felt like they were constellations… we were constellations."

• CARA PAGE •

our egun splay open their wrists & hunt for sapphire—
archaeologists for us, our egun—painting our bodies red
with georgia mud—our egun, menses— flint and knives,
small signs of life—our egun mouths of fire, of flies—
egun like lightening bugs, turning night into a June— trans
forming our many deaths into inheritance—defying
the cleavers and tar, the barbed wire, the boiling oil, the
torch fire, the porch bombs, the addled calls, severed
brake lines or draggings behind wagons, drowned or
thrown down the well—bodies worthy of golden roux,
of promises like *gentle* or *patience* or *free*—worth the
purchase of a plot of land for our bones to rest in—like
our egun we are macheted in two, and even in battle, no
one honors the spelling of our names—my eight letters
an egun's beckon & what lovely sounds to salt a garden
with, to forget their own invention—our egun, trouble—
our egun *trebled*—lifting a chin into a cloud—in other
words, defiance—*gxrl, didja think yaself alone in this room? y'all*
follow us sorrows like a map—our egun, gorgeous
cartographers, hollowing tenderness out into borders—
our egun, a sky drawing it's rivers up from earth—waters
that are only waters and not blood—our people: nine
magnolia seeds, braided cloves of gardenia, reduced
broth—i write egun & mean technology—egun, meaning
multitudes—thousands whose necks were queered into
strange shapes—thousands more caged—a thousand
more still, dead—and sure this could be a eulogy but look

at the life of it all—us, sliding outta english like oil—our
hands cupped to catch their whispered names: *ha iet* , *s jou*
ne , *fan ie* , *ali e*—we breathe unsegregated by time—
integrate to the historic architecture, to our kindred
billions—our egun hold scores of hands—and our hands
contain this book— look: i said contained & could not
mean shackled—contained and there is no iron but the
blood—the blood, unspoiled—the blood unsullied by
clay, by the bark of night—our people growing like
a lineage of trees—poem in which our mouths are
orchards towards the egun—poem in which our people be
a pantheon of articulate beasts—what strange science
makes this possible? for rekia to die in an alleyway and still
give birth to a world—for muhlaysia booker's teeth to be
their own precious alchemy—for egun to be the most
tender name we give our ghosts—commanding blood
to stay in the shape of the stars so we can hold it—in our
bones we call it marrow, in the mouth, manna—true
shape: a mountain spits out from the dirt and we weep—
what god did ta dem, what they done ta each us, gxrl, ain't you as
tired as we?—what industrial magic—brought here in the
trunks of trees and now even the floorboards bend to our
will—our egun a maternal audacity and who we got to
fear? what glory ain't our name? we, a league of soft
warriors, hardened only by soot—*come with we*—by the
river we fashion our enemies into sails, our wildest dreams
into a boat— *c o m e w i t h w e* — o u r bodies *worthy*—
golden roux—our bones rest—*worthy*—for our egun—
          i abandon my heavy. i set this place ablaze.

portrait of rage with caution tape & bullhorns

Erica Garner Will Not Stop Marching
• ABC NEWS •

No matter who we lost, the cab drivers are stiff
in anti-protest. the corrupt streets, like
jails, are in season & exasperated tax dollars do their
thing

our fathers fight to breathe while
we fight the police air, the police rain, the commissioners
the handcuffed ground they died on,
we lie on. We are arrested
in grief & in rage. We fear
we are a national crisis

If our lives mattered, you would vote
us safe. If our lives mattered, you would die
in the name of my father's lungs. If our vote mattered,
we wouldn't
choose presidents, we'd play outside & not
be afraid. The neighborhoods are
overrun by public interests
& what do you want? My father prayed eleven times & still
ain't here

I'd rather be angry, no matter what
it doesn't solve
I'd rather be forgotten than promise you justice
or the end of my mourning
instead imagine a world where my name is my name
& a video is enough evidence

Our men are killed or our daddies are jailed
our mothers rescue our homies from blood
I, too, am killed
stunned or stoned by a million faulted trials
I, too, cannot breathe cannot breathe **cannot breathe** cannot breathe
cannot breathe cannot breathe
cannot breathe **cannot breathe** **cannot breathe cannot breathe**
cannot breathe cannot breathe

He was my father but is no more
& now everything i have is a bullhorn is a father
now the pavement will father me Or my father's
breath will island its way into a mouth, will teach me
how to father myself to death

in honor of my daughter,
I watch my father bellow on national television
and whistle into my hands. It's never really over.

I died twice, truly my father's
daughter and stubborn.
on Tuesdays and Thursdays
i return the boroughs, a body bag and claim the streets in his name

war strategies for every hood

for Dajierra Becton

there we were—laughing cuz we thought there was nothing left
for them to steal. they came back anyway, to take even the mortar
i guess. the creased sundresses on Lowery Blvd, our bean pies

and turmeric milk. the fish trees opening
their blossomed mouths on MLK, for MLK even
for Morris Brown & the Dome. for the tennis courts

on Washington, for Jazzfest & Auburn. or the tiny dance floor
at Department Store, them virgin mojitos one fine ass DJ snuck us
when we were too young to know better & he, old enough to notice

someone stole our grandmothers' laundry carts & charged us
to rent them back by the hour. & every other hour they bombed
another neighborhood. gave it leftover letters from places they ruined: *SoMad, WeHo, WestMar*

they came for the AUC, unearthed bricks lining our streets like copper bullets
they came to drive the corner preachers over county lines. the prostitutes
too & when our daughters left the house, they returned to us soaking. wet
rows of hair missing from their young scalps. backs purpled by the knees of policemen.

not long before now, what little they allowed us learn,
we learned. whatever corner they gave us for us, we kept for us
stayed among the borders they drew round our bodies & swaddled our babies
in red ink. now what? they came bringing shiplap and measuring tape
they filled our mouths with saltwater, our pools with teeth
they came to turn our wounds into deeds, our rubble to profit, and they did

& now what? now what? now what? now what?
what now? now what? now what? now, what? *what now? what now? what now?*

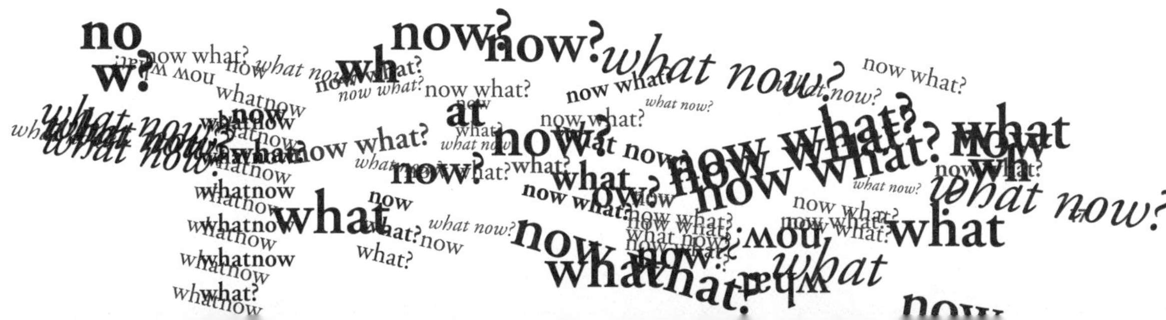

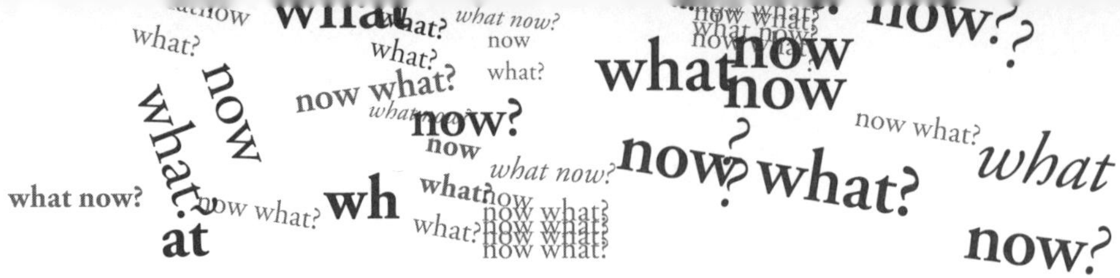

the night after our evictions we were no more
than petty cash offers, liens, dethroned ghetto kings
our delicate empires gutted by quiet legislation
*a condition of battl*e, they called it, *precautionary measures*

we do what little we have left to do: slit the braids from our scalps
twenty inches at a time, whittle our nails into daggers, and march. we
lure policemen into narrow alleys and from behind them, rope hair
from our fists unto their necks. *a condition of battle. precautionary measures.*

from out our homes, flood their pleading faces. gentrifiers
bartering for mercy with china from our mothers' closets
but we war blood now, cashed our mortgages in for machetes and kanekalon
our braid lynch cords slip into loops around their necks. held taut for small eternities
& then, finally let slack. over & *a condition of battle. precautionary measures* over & *a condition of battle*
precautionary measures over

for our niggas, our mothers, our hood
we sang
for our daughters
our daughters
our daughters.

i, too, sing america

don't hold me, don't hold me when niggas is dying
• NONAME •

so, here's the truth:
Black as ever.

Black   and on my knees before an old friend
             his mouth open
             his head coiled and crooked
             his toes too. eyes closed

Black   and he look dead and i at his feet
             but he not.   i wipe my mouth. i keep him alive.

here's the gods-honest truth:
as Black as it is heavy.

Black   and he did die, eventually
             left my house, hungry and expiring of thirst
             drew his hood to keep what was left dry, dry
             walked too fast in a place that wasn't his

Black   and filled with familiar wounds
Black   and left me a widow of sorts
             i gnashed my teeth. i tore my robes
             there was no choice but to mount a pig's head on a stick
Black   and setting flame to tarmac
             eating teargas and the blues

        among the legends   i am asked to recount him
i wipe my mouth.   i keep him alive.

~~no name in the street~~

they called him Money
& he had none. ion even
gotta tell you how funny that
aint. they called him June
mint or, that June, he tasted of
pepper. i forget. i remember
they called his hands to the front
the smoke was thick &
the bullets carved—
no. he had a name. i think
it was dark & my mouth
let out a sound & suddenly
there he was. grinning over
the sound of artillery &
bruise-laughter. *you rang?*
& i never asked for help
but i ended up saved. anyway
someone told me he died
casually. like the world
swallowed his noise & gave
us the broth to recall him by.
i laid with him & never
told no one. never called him
nothing but a cool blush of smoke.
he asked me to gift him a way
out, a name to be welcomed home
inside & i couldn't offer anything up,
not even all me. anyway.
someone told me he died
casually. i called him up
& ask *is it true?* he say something
bout there being no war in the blues.
he aint answer my question. directly

after, the whole room got to
smelling like pepper. like June.
gun powder in a Ferguson
sky. & i be damned. there aint
no word to call this what it is

gxrl gospel ii: when thrown against a sharp white background

after Morgan Parker
after Glen Ligon
after Zora Neale Hurston

I always *feel* Black, y' know? | I close my eyes at night & the tar behind them lids | ain't nearly as dark as me | I wake to a thousand white daggers

darting ocular | *Its only sunlight baby* my lover laughs | I wanna feel most colored when my lover calls me *baby* | her eyes quelled

into half-moons | Instead | my color join us in the aisle @ Target | a white man barreling toward us | & spits | *Nigger Dykes* he say

& I'm all *Yea? Ok But You Ain't Gon Beat My Ass!* | I tryna avoid incarceration & it ain't working | Or *it* is | I refuse to elegy & I'm grow-

ing weary of fighting | I am knuckled into concrete white schools | Is mine a body kept alive by white repute? | some of the poets call these

jails | and others *pipelines*, or *warzones* | I'm inclined to agree | I been told I got *promise* when I write | about fucking| instead of bullets| *Promise*

meaning a poem so beautiful, I must not be *tragically Black* | however drowned I am | by white noise | when calling for help | an officer arrives,

his gun drawn at me while my weapon melts | I mean, my mouth leaks blood | Am I armed, then | or, breathing? | Am I a threat to the nation

or a small nation of risk | or a threat to a nation of risks | or any way, an inconvenience | Colored | Loud | Or colored? | I am sharpened

against | a flint of white rage | Or *how dare you say women & exclude the white ones* | I'm fighting the idea of *police* & *fathers* | Or else I am dreadful &

mad | I'm salacious & ever stuck on old shit | or a shitty writer | Perhaps it's true | Perhaps I feel
my nigga & | color it but what I mean is

I'm cocky | I think I know betta | the Target security guard walks us to our car | says women like
us have to be *discreet* | I'd like to think he meant

safe | I feel most colored when I realize it's dangerous | to explain myself | casually | I feel most
colored | when someone make it clear

ain't nothing bout me *relaxed* | It ain't simple: I'm colored & proudly line my bed with women |
which is perhaps the saddest | Blackest praise |

I'm colored *bitch* or *baby* | in the streets | I critique colored | I color formally | I form the poem |
poem the critic | I flint or fleck color

I set it aflame | I perform white | into a bed and fuck it | I'm dirty after | I don't shower | I call
the police | pigs | & build my politic

in jazz | I dance wild | *don't touch the floor issa jungle* | I have no race & this ain't my country|
ain't got skin in it | I'm so dark | I'm the cosmos

& | you can't catch the Blues or pronounce my name without biting your tongue | don't touch |
can't feel me | less you colored

like me | can't pin me to a wall | or chain my hands to my feet | or make me translate | you can't
even see me | I'm so colored, I'm

invisible | I widen my legs & disappear | you think you shutting | my mouth | you just endorsed
my shit | feel me? | against a wall

I am colored & | *This A Stick Up* | against her chest I am colored | *Oh Please, Oh Yes* |
When I beg I'm colored | When I'm broke

too | when I have children | when my womb is barren | I'm so nigga, I ain't got no name |
I answer to the titles of books

Call me *heavy* | Or *magic* | Or *achilles*
Call me *bestiary* | Or *homie*
| Or *hull.*

gxrl gospel iii: marigold

okay, yea i got some chedda chompas! so
what? i'm yuck mouthed
but i smell good. i love me, unto the very
tooth of the thing—
my crooked, crooked mouth of daffodil
enamel, school buses bitin the half
of a sun, yellow & i guess
i still sing, cuz i am a bird
or perhaps, its god. my eye rests
upon my own self, clockin. i be as sure
as the second hand. me, a metronome & i
masturbate in my mother's heels, laugh
the print of my thumb into my softest
fool parts. oooo, i love me so
dangerous! i could live forever, like this here. a hazard in
heels, naked and sprawled wet
with sin. Black as in what it means to touch a
belly & rejoice: oh, god. oh, me.
oh, yes. damn I'm slick! damn, i spill the thick of me
and it is not blood. i'll say it as many times as i see fit. Oh,
the possibilities of being ego. thank you
for giving the poet somethin
to hunger after. a place to kick off her shoes. i
protest in the tradition of fugitive
poetix: my hand holding tight
my other hand between my thighs.
Yes, this here a freedom song. i know
not why a caged bird
would ever sing my name

transhistorical for the x in my gxrls

for Nani and Sophia, for Brontë, for Sentura,
for Nabi and urrbody wit an x

v.

i too/ have wasted my magic
escaping the focus
of white male insecurity
like a liar i've called it
supremacy/ it makes me no more
a fool than it makes them god
what's in a name?

i was still born and limp
at my birth/ labored
from this jaw
comes a new sound/ *womxn*
in lieu of bitch
                    gxrl/ an entendre
untethered from the gut/ of men

vii.

as far as births are
concerned/ first there was Phillis
then other griots followed
like a bloodlet/ another one there
climbing through the window
of an ivory tower/ more of them
afterward/ in darker
and darker droves

i am of a riot/ bastard tongue/ born
writhing in the *both/and* practically
illegible in multiplicity/ where two or more
are gathered it is my mouth
sneering/ into the margin's margin
i write hungrily/ a mastication

once/ i read of a writer
named Dove/ and envisioned myself
flying/ then a gxrl like me/ Lovelace
i rename myself a bound book
somewhere/ a library weeps with sudden
pages of shocking Black flesh
a white man told me my literacy
was a failure/ and perhaps it was [his.]

iii.

if i wasn't here
if i had not survived
this country/ what
would white women have
to create themselves with

i find antithesis to be a powerful origin

[see here/ i am *not* a monster
i have *no* fangs/ have killed no one
nor prayed into the mouths of men]

a white woman ain't me
and so must be her smallest self
which is to say *i am/ that i am*
you is/ whatever i've left to rot

which of us becomes the fable
if the other disappears?

viii.

whereas the *i* can only attest
and x consents to none of it
each violence assigned
at birth/ the genital matter bloodied into a name
what's in a name?
i witness/ *i* is complicit and so allows
x into the soil/ sows possibility and mud

i chews
i swallows
becomes
gxrl [here*!*] [here*!*] [here*!*]

i.

god ain't no different than *gxrl*
marrow of stars alive in our hands
magical/ terrified/ sovereign

our names our own/ finally
iron-soiled/ brimming
with the curse of silt/ *what's in them names*
conjurers or architects?

gxrl as in/ a whole world
made flesh of our dark flesh
we call it rootwork/ this building
each new break
wielding a god body

vi.

i like simple violence
cesura-ed into fiction
and *x* the Black
rhetorical/ christ conjuring

[does the author consider this art
catastrophe or crucifixion?]

not to say i am god/ but to imply
i been left/ to fester in the sun
like a sore for a city

folk gather at my palms to view
they own holes/ wounds to mark
where myths entered/ where disgust made exit
hole in our skulls perhaps imagined/ body
whittled into petit metaphor
cast in bronze/ wrapped in barbed
teeth/ pocket body
barely even a name to hold
the flesh to bone yet/ holy

ii.

they pulled me from my almighty mother
and the doctors couldn't find my face
smacked their palms against my bloody
flesh to see which end

of me made the most noise
followed the cord that tethered
my mother to me and discovered a neck
strangled/ nutrient dense leather

gargled and gargoyled i fought/ for air
and so yes/ my birth was not
unlike a lynching

my mother weeping/
surrounded
by men readying their knives to harvest parts of me
if ever i gave/ up the struggle
hours-long was this fight for life my little heart blistering
into bloom. the story hasn't changed

iv.

what i mean is this/ country
is mine if only because
from my mouth i spit its loam
and unspin a noose/ i won't exploit my name
the only metaphor i was given
instead/ i hunt/ for x/ for vicious
edges/ and build myself a muse

yes/ i earned this country
i owe it nothing
with my infinite infant hand
i manipulated/ death sentences
into a single compound-complex one

out the umbilical/ i bled/ a life worth writing
down/ and in a century's time there will be another
word created still for subversion tactics in/ the unaming
the alternative alchemy/ a Black gxrl's first breath.

& not by sight

every year I stretch wider.
my arms streetlights, my tongue
stubborn gardenia. my hips suddenly exhaust
the doorframe to my grandmother's
kitchen. I crumple my childhood home
beneath my heel. what a queer sorrow, this nostalgia.
I cluck my tongue and cicadas fall from their nap,
inconveniencing July. the year turns its stomach.
my father adds another bullet to the mouth
of that vintage trumpet. my mother grows a third
set of teeth. I am unsure
of the creature waiting to be freed
from beneath my scalp. what is this beast
my brother wrestles into shadow
above my bed? come, summer. I'll play
the anthem of my kin. as many cousins
as a season's yield of blue crab, divided
by the sum of wives my grandaddy kept
at once. I hate the skin of peaches,
the smell of nectar. everything men lust after.
I keep my legs closed, and still, cannot
please my aunts. I hold my tongue until it break
loose I pray for my own sake
I name whoever answer me

God

the creek behind my childhood home was one of those small heavens

and i often would come
offering pebbles or disassembled frogs
my earnest, most blue haint prayers:

oh child river
            of my meek mouth and splintered home
you quiet moisture in the sand

            Are all these openings, wounds?

& what is a heaven without a god to break it

there was th time
he came spinnin
wildly from th
bowel of a car
n 2 your mother's choir director's
livin room reekin of selfpity & a
woman
name Akeela
his hands some ugly
inertia pullin all four
uh you out onto th
cold pavement
mother fucka thought
you wasn't gon swing

some of the men we love are terrorists

Some begged, some climbed the side of my body looking for a window,
some said they were on their way and did not come.
• WARSAN SHIRE •

& honestly, i have no solutions—our world a mad swarm of bees. forgive me my own devotion, the handsome clench. my first love masters a sinister arithmetic; his patrilineage swelling like a heavy god between his legs. i'm well-conditioned, my hands already working for the good of this sly new lord. blessed are the meek. at one point, i was a brief globe of possibility & then my father got to me. have i the option to love him, my mother's delicate monster, & not write this poem? of course not. it is a woman's mouth, after all, bleeding nuance into the Ferguson pavement. the relevance, this; her bruises born of a husband's impatience, muddled by police batons. i imagine it less & less possible, then—black as i am, woman in the small places they count, to be in love & not articulating war. my body no one's patriot, nor my blood, artillery. i wound my own hands.

i'm afraid

of what's true: there is no one left to rescue, yet i love each my father's mirrors. in the name of salvation, the saying goes, *some of the men*, we love. and yes, i glory his mouth. which of *the men we love, are terrorists?* the first time my lover coiled his fist to quarry me from my bone, i knew there must be a church in my father's name, filled with womxn like me &

i pay my tithe

father-son & holy

after Audre Lorde

my father ain't dead
                    yet.
I kiss him & smell his flesh
waitin to gangrene.
my father's hands be the hands
of small tyrants. he inhabit
power in measures of three
welts fadin sweetly
'cross a daughter's cheek—not
to claim my father hit me—

'less he found mind to. mother to toddler, I un
string his shoes at the evenin
        his face pained with the day's
        yellowed failure. *You a mighty*
        man, I coo to him, strokin the greyed
        scalp, skin pricklin with dead growth.
I'm tired he sigh, and I abandon
my study. *I'm lonely* he say, and I
forsake the world. *I'm hungry* he cry,
and I slice my body
                    into fleshy ribbon
& sauté him a feast.

each week   I'm a different woman
        brown as them forty-ounce bottles
        he hide clumsily in his pocket or
        coy & delightin in hand games or
        fascinatin a habit of fixin his children up
        up up up   then tearin us to pieces,
                                        briar by briar

each week   I saunter into his kitchen
          score my body & ruin my appetite
each week   I'm a new bitch
          i try on my mama's
          apron   *it never fits*

my father lives in a home I built.
fingers a trumpet I made out my teeth.
my father fashion a song out himself so well
I know the words. I sing to him. he fight sleep.

this was once my mother's job
and now, I ain't got no momma. she somewhere
dancin with new face. i could never call her,
a mother-child. what for? my mama never asked me
to help raise her.   not even from the dead

unholy ghazal

there simply is no blasted God—there is only man and it is he who makes miracles
• L. HANSBERRY •

I have my convictions: no one watches over sparrows. In my mother's house there is somehow a God
who listen to me blaspheme. I tell the truth about my own magics, and anger my mother's iniquitous God

I sharpen prayer into knives and kneel only for pleasure, now that I know better. My mother
says I will fall ill or get caught up in revolution, and realize the sovereignty of her disastrous God

But thirteen died in a chapel searching for *his* glory, and elsewhere, a 13-year-old was killed during bedtime
prayer, her hands pressed to her chest, eyes looking up and I assume she was calling upon some just God

I sat in a paddy wagon after that, sure of my death, my hands tied to my feet, my feet tied to the floor
I am sure in that moment, my mother prayed, but instead I sang. Yes, the songs were my faultless God

I crooned at the top of my lungs until my voice broke. Instead of beating me, the police, they
laughed. They forced quarters into my mouth, requested their favorite songs, their notorious

God of Abraham, fear was greater than you. My own two wrists that I broke to slip the cuffs, too
were bigger Gods by their own circumference. My mother's God fit in my pocket. My pouch God,

waited until the coast was cleared to show his face. The first sounds he chewed into a word—*Sorry.* & I am
too, you God of ruin. God of dead children, and of the police. & oh, of my mother, too. A heinous God.

yes, i am done with the god of white men

I chose instead the soft curdling holy of my roommate Che
who bends themself into glory before an altar + nine cool jars

water pools and nips of whiskey + yes I'd rather praise a sovereign drunk
or my petty + glorious + dead brother who never brushed his teeth

I am no longer offering my earnings tax-free to your so-called
divine one + I trust his funk less than I trust a policeman at my back

+ we know that's the same thing right? you wake up on Sunday
dress your children in my mother's toil + even then I don't

trust your god with kids + I think of my Aunt Deborah +
her body + riddled with good + how I cried for her

when she caught your god's holy like the plague + Grown enough
for the revival that year + I finally learned how many ribs I carried

beneath my chest + let the minister's son trail his hand
across them + if your god is the god of practice then I am the god

of exploration + I am the god of finding names for all the places
our bones meet + the god who solves the mystery of an appendix

last august and every summer + your god let the black boys
leak from the knees of the clouds + like cartilage you could say

they were born for this + but I saw one go right in front of me on Lowery Blvd
a tennis racket in his limp hand + one eye toward the heavens + the other

bulleted to pieces above the gutter + His strange body shook
from me my peace + a memory of my aunt Deborah moaning

your god's name like a scorned lover + her tongue bloodied on
his robe + I would've kept screaming *don't die, don't die* to him

But a white man said *you're blocking the lane* + I caught my hands holding
each gasp at the joints + From outside my body, my body heard me wail

+ this is the work of your silly god + now the boy is gone + your god is murderous
I wept Deborah's name + her body missing + your god probably stole that too

I don't trust him to watch over us without taking your bribes + I don't
trust him to not play devil's advocate + I don't trust your god

to refrain from hunting us down, don't trust he'll resist the urge to stuff us
full of white folk, Get Out style + I think your god is trippin + I think you got stuck

with an immature holy + I think your god just got here + they's playing catch up
I think your god tricked his way into power + I've never prayed well to frauds

gxrl gospel iv: beast of a southern wild

even my father fell for it, forgot I was
softened and fragile. my mother too—
so consumed in her grief that she never stopped to ask
where the rage in me was born & so could,
for the purposes of this poem, be considered dead—

GUNS! GUNS!
GUNS! GUNS!

once, without consenting, i cleaned the mess my father made
of my mother, her lipstick spilled terribly across the black windows
of his mistress. which of these women was the animal? Look:
a daughter plans a wedding and a funeral with no tears

SHOW ME YA GUNS!

I never could prove I wasn't leaking from
these familial wounds when I finally found creatures
similar to me, holdin the names of other womxn in they jaws
like blessed oil. I discovered myself softly, and *like a freedom too queer*
felt myself suddenly naked in sin, or, more openly, pleasure.

LEMME SEE EM.

bi, as in where two or more are gathered in my name
bi, as in where the sweat pools and i find myself unafraid
bi, as in my father punished me like a mirror
bi, like i want to expand, expand, expand
bi, meaning opposite of scarcity
bi, as in i cum in many languages, for several breeds of tongues

AND WHAT I SAY?
NO CRYING!

I was 8 and longing rolled beneath me a world of its own, soft
as the belly of a magnolia leaf. nobody put my body
on a ballot, yet I been told my ancestors died for it.
my only option has been to build the magic
I yearned for, create the things
                    i couldn't see

THIS COUNTS AS I'M SORRY
FOR A WHOLE BUNCH OF THINGS, LORD

transhistorical and i observe the Sabbath like a ill verse

she made a church out of feathers . . . she gave my name away, to your holy house
• NONAME •

vi.

my mama's love be a mountain high in flight
i build her a house at the foot of my bed
          these be the truths   we bore together   as a tamed bruise

i.

i do not believe in my mother's god
          but i do   believe   my mother
          when she tell me all things work for the good
                              of those who love the lord
          &   i love my mama
          where are my good things? i know who gave me my name

iii.

               my mama
a church of feather and sweat above my lip
an ocean in neglect
a decent god. a faith in bruises. she who sours
at the dawn, abashed in her mourning & still
               trusts a word like salvation

ii.

my mama
is   my god
i watch her eat this life's emptiness, an almighty tithe
my god
          lords over my hands, this sanctuary made in her likeness
and already yearning for gold
my god has tamed the edge of heaven
my god the gutter after a storm,
 her rage broken
          into   my rib,

v.

i prepare a table in the company of
eviction notices
anoint my own head with the day's blood dew
i cannot drown in the oceans my mother
has wept for me
my god called forth
from her own body, an aquifer
without her, what would I have left to drink?

iv.

i sing my mother's praises
into the mouth of
three sparrows and everything
in these prayers
be a feast

i n d e p e n d e n t

My momma was a grocery //
+ broth //
My momma full us //
a witch of water + salt //

gangster, could feed her kids with leather //
the swollen meat of her right hand //
My momma fool us //
O what terrible magics //

i too heal my younger self here + yearn

for the touch //
but it wasn't// enough //
+ into // a cast iron //
made into the stickiest tough //
tricks of saints //
of money // things I wanted + did not //
I ain't have //
the men who too, wanted //
//

a hem // her sweat a feast
to sing // dew from the ground
that last meal stretched for two weeks //
the stuff of legends //
+ I knew better // than ask //
know better than wanting what //
I wanted + ain't want to want them //
+ did not want to // be seen in their aching

but did so desire // me + found //
desire thirsting like deserts
my broth with a slick //
I thought my hips
young witch of water
my momma's first //
to never want // for what I could not

themselves wandering // my thighs //
for want // I found them // + earned //
boil of sweat + whatever //
could do at sixteen //
+ sulfur //
born of desire + a desire //
craft // in my own hand //

listen,

I've released the fish back into the ocean
In his mouth, one hook and my earliest memory

I named the fish after my father and did not kill him.
See me in all my forgiving glory!

The fish gill slit and sly, slip skinned and slutty
My father, wearing a different beast's hide

I snuck an oyster blade into its eye, and that was all: I am not exempt
from attempts at blind rage. I am indeed my father's daughter.

A fisherman's muse. A flounder's second chance at swim.
If there was a storm, I would've taken it as a sign,

but the natural order isn't equipped for revenge.
No, the sky was bursting with the *possibility* of rain

and the fish had my father's eyes. So away he went, half blind
and still unable to speak my name across the bar I caught him in

tangled up between the holes of a net, or a woman who was not my mother.
I shouldn't abandon the metaphor, for your sake, but my father

was a promiscuous man and I don't know if any fish has left
his young to starve, or fall victim to the vacuum of a whales mouth.

Besides, here is a trout or a perch or a snapper, maybe, his fin
flecked toward my blade, so-called scales illuminate in the sun

and fuck if I am not trying to be a different breed of man.
I am trying to improve upon my paternal line. I am empathetic

enough to the aquatic, more than I am given credit for. I have
not done unto a scaled belly, what has been done to mine.

I hate a thing without gutting it. I can love a father
& never lie about what I do with my knife when he leaves

a poem of failures

an unresolved sestina is a father

finally, the seasons switch they tempo. pollen brings us back to life
our lungs trippin on marigold and silt. children make angels in the dander + ain't
nobody thinkin bout dyin yet. all this to say, I been
tryna find a way to tell my father his life wasn't no
gospel, but saved me just the same. I mouth Langston's last song into a crystal
vase, weep silently into my hands. I'm still waitin to bloom, right here on the 11th stair.

early June flexes her joints + I pass blood, avoid men who stare
at my lil chest from behind they wives' fingers. womxn who dun soiled whole lives
of possibility, tryna polish a dagger of a husband into love. crystalline
shards live where glory once did, in they fingers. I kno that story. it's my mother's. I ain't
lyin—I was young then. a gxrl-child as green + fertile as the ends of dandelions. no,
I wasn't holy. my father scolded me into the leather at his waist, said *shouda been*

memorized the blues, maybe that woulda closed ya legs. I'm bein
hyperbolic, of course. he began this a ritual to shame the honeysuckle outta me. used a stair
well to slip one generation's horror into the next, almost magic. made us chew psalms for supper. I kno
the way it sound. a grown ass man, forcin his daughter's mouth round a live
thing, a sorrow too old for her young body. this ain't
that, I swear. this is me paintin a mural of my father from memory. tryna keep it all crystal

clear. his life depend on it. I love a man I'on truly understand, understand? I crystallize
him in black + half-truths. try to write his palm flatter than it was + who that benefit
most? here's the truth: I hate you for what you did to my mother + what you ain't
do for me. I love you for pullin oyster knives out your bones, sterilizin
them for me to make use of later. you stirred red clay + a dark bruise into some kinda life
+ I tell myself it was all for posterity. here's truth: I lie + say this for me, but we both know

I'm tryna tell you somethin I can't reach, no
matter how many poems I write. each time the sun crystals
across your hands on the southwest side—docile + brewin coffee—I weep. what a life
you've pulled from the hip of mud. once it was ash, then a ghost, now sage. you been
the altar + the witching hour. you've tossed my mother down stair
ways clear 'cross the county. once my mouth bled for three days on the hem of your fears + ain't

it funny? I wouldn't kno you now. do I call that growth or anti-climactic? I ain't
afraid to say I'm afraid to love you. I ask God to shed light on the matter + She gon say *no*
matter what you forgive, how you gon resolve it to the bone + what is prayer but a failure to stand, anyway? I stare
back at the fingers of my father, decide to wipe them clean. drench them in honeydew + laugh
grief pools like a wound that yields no
blood + a father is a sinner or a 2008 Chrysler
+ a father is a suture or saving no one's life
+ I finish the work without knowin
that this ain't
how it ends + the poem threads my hand to the bottom of the stair

held like arsenic in each my kin's mouths

gxrl, he musta lost his mind
down souf wit dem whyt girls
an all'at reefer

musta lost his
damn mind

shole did!

last I seent him,
started talkin bout
eyes made of drones
an blood in my teef when I
aksd him how he wuz feeling

da nerve

an 'nem walls
didja hear about
they walls?

mmm, gurl

wut walls?

X, aint you say
is momma tole you
he say he heard voices
up in da plaster

from da horses
mouth haself

Lord, Xora Day!

Im jus sayin
she tole me he took
a hammer to da hole place

. . . an her too
or so I heard

well aint dat
a shame

unh huh

how you hea dat part?

she tole 'Tricia den
Tricia tole Leonard
an Leonard tole me

my my my

well you know
he took da car

from rite up unner
his momma in da dead of nite
drove ta Santa Barbara ta
live on a beach

unh huh,
takin by force wut
no one gave him
in da firss place

ha'mercy lord

dat boy jes like
his daddy
afta all

dass rite.

well—
an is you surprised,
wit a momma like that?

prone ta leavin they daddy
in da dead of nite

sittin jobless in Decatur
of awl places

Decatur?

chile, aint eem
no beach

i tole him to watch who he
lay down wit, watch who he rear
children wit. now look

well nawl, hol'on . . .
ain't she say he usta
beat ha?

. . . he couldna hit ha
mo den twice, ion thank

mm,
mm
mm

wemmen ain't werf
they snuff no mo

I ain't
neva like
dat gurl,
now she wit
a whyt man

ta beat it awl!

an dat lil heffa she
raise nearly wild
outchea marchin

an carryin on
belly hangin
over ha draws
kissin on sum otha gxrl
like she ain't no chile uh god

lord, ha'mercy

they muss be somethin
triflin up in dat house

downrite bewitchin

caint we do sumn?

nawl
the LORD dont give
more den wut you can stand
they be alrite

a crazy, a lesbian,
an wut da third one up to?

community college?

Nawl, state schoo

unlikely. motherin like dat
dont lead you no whea but hell

aintchu say they daddy
usta be sumthin of a
tyrant?

well nawl
thas my brother.
he did da bess he cud.

CPT or lessons in god-timing

wait i have
only bought
into your god
for his taste
in *wait* music
i come *wait*
with my *wait* legs *wait* closed
wait to feel
stirred *wait*
by sound
how great *wait*
what art
the sound
my holy *wait*
is a black
wait gxrl who says
my name
wet *wait* a thursday
morning *wait* i borrow
your broke ass *wait*
gods to try out
other drunken joys
wait i praised her
like *wait* my mother
does, the god of *wait* Abraham *wait*
with open arms and *wait* a song
my thighs *wait* parted by tides
I am wet
with a sickled *wait*
sin. what's mine
in the garden
of eden if i *wait* am wanted

wait by adam,
if i walk
with the snake *wait*
if i lay
with eve & *wait* then her man
what's my name
i love gxrl-god.
i love the *wait* mess
she *wait* makes
of me love *wait*
how the *wait* ruining
feels. I run into *wait*
fields of salt *wait*
i am sin
scoured i *wait* fall
to my knees
in *wait*
worship
i flee
wait i fling
i flicker *wait*
i flittle
wait i speckle
i feck
wait i fraud *wait*
i force *wait* i fringe
i fray
i wait i wait, i wait

gumbo ya ya

It is important, Sisters, that you understand what gumbo ya ya means. . . .
A cacophony of sound, like a swarm of bees, is moving in my direction.
• MADAME LUISA TEISH •

the original metric for rigor was
a single torso of wood, made boat, stuffed
full of our mothers and our sons. no matter.
it was only our ending.
it is how our story begins. every poem either
breathes it, or buries it. don't worry, i am not
here to make a citizen's arrest
i don't believe in the jails or
form, but i believe in the freedom of breaking

this is a simple poem about criticality, reader. i promise.
          the pure animal of labor, or honest hustle. what it takes
to turn a woman into a mule, and then a man, and then a match

heifer was my mother's name before she made me.
my mother is no thief, though the product of it. my mother gave
birth to marauders. my mother came here to cash
this speech in for fresh vegetables. I was only allotted
my time. I was instructed to say thank you. gratitude is tricky math.
I'd like to thank the academy for carving open my head. I'd like
to thank the academy for splitting my tongue
I recognize that my work is all gristle, thank you, america
for stealing the meat.   what's the pronunciation of my name?

/ / /

dis shit hard & it fly
bout as far as I can
throw da pen
my mouf slip & I rig
or wring my jaw into chrome

spinners, the asphalt melts
& i chew tobacco. that first
summa is where we left it
out to dry & damn i said what the
fuck i said. i neva stutta less
we talking clarity. i say i write gully &
mean i write the wing back onto the
bird. the bird
a limp thing & i said it before

at the pussy march, the women were bitches
my bitches marched, some without pussies
some of my bitches, ain't. just like that.
i, she-bitch, birthed megaphones
the women held their purses in the downbend
of their mouths— away from us, they kept their children & the keys to the city
their pussies fists, closed. their backs turned, refusing to meet our eyes.

all the names they shouted
was our names.
all the gxrls they chanted was our gxrls:

Mercedes Successful, Atattiana, Mya, Sandra, Ayana Stanley's
sweet seven year old body, Rekia Boyd and her skull-hole,
Tanisha, Shelley Frey. Alexia Christian, her hands with more
wounds than a certain messiah. Natasha McKenna, Tarika Wilson,
Kayla Moore, Malissa Williams, Miriam Carey, we sang Shantel
Davis like an aria, and Kendra James too. Duanna Johnson's we
whispered like a secret and oh, our gxrls our gxrls our gxrls. our
gxrls our gxrls our gxrls our gxrls. our gxrls. our gxrls. our gxrls.
our gxrls. ours.

despite them singing us out like war songs they treated us like paupers
their money, our blood. they knit and we bled. they chanted and our bodies
stretched for miles,
foot by hand

/ / /

[*If an understanding of Blackness is as an entity that defies whiteness, is either killed by it or surviving from it, or is perpetually either reconsidering or fracturing what whiteness normalizes, how does one disrupt what we may assume is the aspiration of Black Poetix?*]

/ / /

I ain't said it yet
but the mouth is a scythe I
ain't gon tell you how But I
break
what english cain't repair
into a slice a thunda
I be's myself, den I be's
a net of small blade

/ / /

[intersectionality]

A Murder of Crows, a Gang of Black Bois
Alternative Title: Ars Poetica & the Things We Are Organized Into [or, Jails]

/ / /

Filia Filia Filia
Filia Filia Filia
Filia Filia Filia
Filia Filia Filia
Filia Filia Filia
Filia Filia Filia
Filia Filia Filia
Filia Filia Filia
Filia Filia Filia
Filia Filia Filia

/ / /

[*but is a manuscript praxis?*]

innovation in the name of Eugene B. Redmond

reader, consider the kwansaba: poem in which you celebrate all the Black you either is or ain't:

/ / /

[see also:]

i. I have only my two hands bloodied
into their rawness marrow my
hands, mirror-hands stethoscopes,
suture hands imparticular structure
I am broken! Praise, my sisters
have broke me open!

ii. for us there is no wrong cure
these hands hold the bodies
we own, our mouths ironsmiths
melding us a world of glass

and bone and sassafrass
and then of course the boat to reach my
sisters who break me open!

/ / /

[*if I put a gun to your head, could you explain how this is not a book about race?*]

Born spineshudder Born
wild
Born dead   The black
gxrl
Born   bulletscissor   Born
throatthread Sinspun
She ain't black gxrl
is, in fact deadgrout
is ghoulgrit is
ironbutter is oakstain
is unhung

Is four years old.

/ / /

Don't Talk To Me About Cruelty Or What I'm Capable Of

/ / /

[*if i put a gun to your head*]

i imagine and acknowledge a future iteration of reality that thrives without a dependence on racialized, gendered, economic oppression. I don't know what it looks like. Has anyone ever written a poem without being told it was possible? Could the rest of the world receive it?

/ / /

[could you explain?]

& this is how I know white
women cherish their tears
above my life:

/ / /

[*intersectionality:*]

I SAID NO
HE FUCKED ME ANYWAY
THIS AIN'T AN ORIGINAL STORY
I STOLE IT FROM MY AXNTIE AND MY SXSTER
FROM SO MANY WOMXN
THAT THIS POEM AIN'T LONELY
JUST SAD

/ / /

[intersectionality:]

i was having lots of orgasms on the bathroom floor   but still
                                        i cannot get out
                                of bed i cannot get out
                                of bed i cannot get out
                                of bed i cannot get out
                                of bed i cannot get out
                                of bed i cannot get out
                                of bed

/ / /

[intersectionality:]

this morning, you woke up
and your pussy felt
like someone
else's

/ / /

[intersectionality:]

I'm no girl.

I am an argument
of crows into the evening's face: cloud-
bruised & tryna find something

for my hand to ruin after the call you
ain't never supposed to get I am
a bible filled with stories of sacrifice & no salvation
what with these holy palms & so many, many bodies on
the battlefield I'm here drinking my father's wine
pretending to be grown I'm some
kind of child bride for your evening's entertainment I welt easy
but do not shatter in the rain

/ / /

oh sunday sap oh
syrup slick oh
sinner salve oh
honey child oh
snake blood oh
young liquor
            new drunk
            child whiskey

i call to you
marrow of some strange christ
mother of all the hood gatherings

/ / /

[*if I put a gun to your head, could you explain how this is not a book about race?*]

DRAFT: Marie penned one selfishly indulgent, self-navigated analysis of the complexity of black "girlhood" in both an intimate and historically placed context: state-sanctioned and intra-communal violence, bilingualism (the Creole of English and southern Ebonic), *sexuality* (what queerness can and cannot be, to the great granddaughter of the enslaved, the granddaughter of sharecroppers), *womanism* (the relationship between a headstrong, quickmouthed gxrlchild and a man-run world, with all its violences . . . specifically, her father's + held in juxtaposition to the feminisms of white women, their pride held like guns against her temple, their hands holding, literally, guns to her temple), *the curiosity of magic* (how ritual folds itself into the mundane), *and a juvenile exploration in intimacy as a simulation of other radical praxes.*

/ / /

& here the proof:
my mother sings again of caged birds
and is one no longer. my father weeps
at the sight of bruise.
My brother is dead
but talks just the same.
The youngest has found his head and again, his body.

/ / /

[*we're just worried that it won't translate . . .*]

> **"It's so wrong," she said. "Think about all the times you're at home, sitting on the couch, watching Netflix, and you heard something. It could have been anybody. She wasn't doing anything wrong. I can't even say 'wrong place, wrong time,' because she was in her house."**

every time i shrink away, i become a
knife spinning open our wounds

/ / /

the opposite of flying is
death the opposite
of falling is death
the opposite of death
is a skinned knee and only a skinned knee

oh summer, oh summer, i claim
the swollen air & i am denied.
i bury my young pulpy brothers in a blanket
& kiss them goodbye.
even with a clear heaven over my head,
even as the sun bears upon us her brilliant mouth

I imagine this is why Tamir
mama cries, her disbelief slick in its torrents.
A hand raising toward the window
A suspicion that God is
laughing

/ / /

i mean gumbo ya ya
i mean no soup for your mouth
but sustenance in a new world
i mean *take from me my breath but never my audacity*
i mean we don't die
i said we don't die
we just multiply

gumbo ya ya and
i do mean whatever the fuck a body does—
dancing into a void, a joyful noise.
a mournful smile. a body slack
or slickened at the opposite end of a line
break tradition

& become the whole Black dirt
beneath my nail, a sound
so smooth it's harlem. it's an island
off the coast of the carolinas. its christmas.
i'm holy

This here is a freedom song.
I know not why a cage
would ever sing my name.

This here is a freedom song.
I know not why a cage
would ever sing my name.

This here is a freedom
song. I know not
why a cage would
ever sing why a cage
would ever sing why
a cage

would ever sing my name.
sing my name. sing my name.
sing my name. sing my name.
sing my name. sing my name.
sing my name. ***sing my name.***

would ever sing my name.
sing my name. sing my name.
sing my name. sing my name.
sing my name. sing my name.
sing my name. ***sing my name.***

pantoum for aiyana & not a single hashtag

            look!
There go a Black gxrl body still
tethered   to her head

There go a Black gxrl, shirt still dry
no river of marrow or tears
following her up the block
no bile from her head

Can we call her into form? not a river of marrow and small tears
of sweaty fabric, but manna and honeysuckle
from her skull no bile, but beatniks
in bloom. Can we celebrate the child on this side of the grass?

her sweat fabric, honeyed and unmanned
the gxrl young, a fresh world of gardenia
bloom-ing. Can't we celebrate? The child's on this side of the grass!
Open the window and usher in a new god! A breeze

gardenia-young, the gxrl a world made fresh.
in her hands piano keys, sticks of cinnamon gum,
a window into the new. God, an usher opening
a psalm, free to be the thing she was truly made of:

piano keys. In her hands, cinnamon sticks like guns
in the wrong light. Never mind that. Today she lives.
A thing to be freed. Made of psalms, and truly
holy. The gxrl will turn flowers into wine. Spills herself no more

wrong. And today, she lives. Never mind the light
offering summer halo. it is a myth, that we die, anyway. We too
holy. No more spills, no more flowers. From wine, gxrl churns herself a will.
Rises from the concrete, her arms full of clove. Her mother's yard a throne.

Anyway, the myth is that we die. We too, summer offering. Halos
like birds on our shoulders. The gxrl, gardenia, and we planted her
full of clove and her mother. She raises a throne from the concrete, a yard of arms.
The gxrl, a god king. The gxrl, a map of good. The gxrl, a thing worth trending, after all. Just
look!

georgia me

Oh blood mud, ground made rust with the iron of us
Oh foggy symmetric, Oh cataract sky
Oh kinky margins displaced by humidity,
Oh the tricky algorithim, animal and wound

Oh Sunday dresses, stained by Christ, his good marrow
Oh the young grass
Oh baptize me, ruin me, oh cool cerulean clean
Oh praise river, oh sovereign dew
Oh made hole and then whole again

Oh son-gone sermons, oh mourning, oh praise
Oh custom tees, oh last rights, oh embalmed smile, oh memory
Oh memory fading behind the knees at dusk

Oh kisses in empty chapels, mouth upon mouth, in the lap of God
Oh God, Oh yes, silk hands tethered in shag carpet frisk
Oh pleasure. 'Bama boys not worth they mama's labor
Oh playing grown in children's church

Oh generation of eager worship,
One after another fallin in love with a false god
Oh broken curses of the family name

Oh family name
Oh lion oh Israel oh spaniard bastard, indigenous dark
Oh gumbo. Oh massa scraps made harvest.

Oh survival survival survival and only a few scars.

Oh pot deeper than a grandmother's prayer
Oh prayer. Oh black magic. Oh slurped marrow.
Oh Rooster feather. Oh Reading bones. Brick dust. Rosehip.
Oh Indigo. Cayenne. High John.
Oh root. Oh root. Oh the work of conquerors.

Oh whistlebullet. Oh ghost tomb.
Oh hollow saunter in and out the gospel
Oh holy, Oh holy, Oh holy, Oh holy

Oh georgia me, fast gxrl in a too slow town.
too heavy for the air. too free.

like a freedom too strange to be conquered

i pretend to cut my eyes at you in line
                                        waitin
                                        for water
swat your laugh away
from my neck in the hall you
got a mouth that like a 'lil nip
anyway
i change your name in my
journal to Marcus surrounded
by petals
in each, a letter
spelling   out into bloom.
damn.
even here in my
own private truth I can't say yes i love
                                        and it is the
youngest, freshest thang yes i love
                                        and at
the formal we gon dance the way
children dance—bodies rubbin hard
against imagination & bone, pantin
before we even know why, droolin the
lyrics of our mothers favorite poems into
one another's ear—oh,   , yes imma
moan your whole name
into a roll of toilet paper and flush. i
swear, I wanna play house
on the black top. i wanna tell the world about you
& i can't. i wanna tell the world about me but i
ain't met her yet.
i wanna tell the world somethin other
than *ooo Fidel Lee so fine*
man fuck that nigga & his sweaty hands i'd

rather dance in the thursday sun   that is your
name. that is your laugh.
i wanna toil in a queerness that ain't
nobody punch line   & speaking of strike—
somehow it was just the two of us
in a bathroom on the third floor that first time
i wash my hands and keep my eyes out the mirror
auri   you say my name
                                    like a damned flute
auri   & i turn slower than worlds
your lips are there & my lips are there & oh god
i love you i love you i love you & was the freest me   right then

thottin on fountain drive

in may
the heat fester
just ova asphalt
hot

we play rough
outside
the pushas house
a thumpin bunch of brick

the bass
leavin nem speakas
like ghosts
rattlin our bones
fo climbin to high heaven

somebody mama callin
down the block

we all look,
scared we dun missed
a midday curfew
long forgot

ground can't make
it's mind up
sometimes 'is stone,
sometimes 'is tapioca
& blunt ash

neighbor boi
ask me if I
seen a dick befo

& I blush
but I ain't say no

she ain't seen one
neither
but watches her
brother get dressed,
                    envious

wishin the sock
              she had
              tucked behin
              'nem panties
              was flesh

I duck

with her
behin
a bush
silent
as the day moses left it

boi got
fingers
in my
thighs
teeth on
my neck
& heat
everywhere
I shiver

skin
raisin
isself up
like
braile

alluva
sudden is 5pm
& this time
my momma callin

imma be ya man now
shawty
she say fo I go,
tongue trippin ova
hood slurry & boi bite

she kiss me niggahard
hand rough in my braids
like she seen her brother do

her breasts & my breasts
pettin each other,
makin nice
'tween hazy slick

man I swear

I swear

I *swear.*

the world between me is gender

i learned from my daddy
how to make quicksilver
from rotten molar/wound i spin
gold out my own rusty

dagger/embrace like my father,
i slick. i plead/cleave the edge
of a woman/universe
betrayed by my innocent/coy

as in question/invoke i curl
my lips *does it hurt* and i/we whisper
her eyes like rivers purring in pleasure
from my father/i learn this:

how to paw/strike at the terrible
delicate how to unfeather her/my thighs
until she spills, i velvet

her blood/spit i am not
my father's son, but i choose/resign
to mirror him proud/evenly

here: she comes/brings all her honesties
into small flood/quake my hands sticky
with the soup

she hides/neglects me like my father
away from her former/lives
does it hurt she asks
her own young shock/grief spinning like
teeth/wet in my hand

transhistorical for the men we love

iv.

he knew a few cats frm back when snow hit them bluffs
hard enuf to splinter concrete like bone
he dont talk bout them years but i dun seen scars

runnin 'cross his faces like old haints
them wounds. everytime a car engine cough into th mornin
or a mother call for her children at th dusk
somethin darken his whole body up into fury
& ther aint no porch blu enuf to quiet them ghosts

ii.

long 'fo poverty swallow up tha southwest side
we knew kings on every corner who lit th sidewalk
wit urine & magic, or bathed inna hydrant's summer song
they grac'd each juke joint door like cathedrals wit pipe glass
& th nights was all hymnals at th neck ov a bottle
back home they aint no such thing as a ghetto or domestic violence.
All th sons of men were heirs of hood glory but us women inherit
always th bruises & bills.   *this here was th world b'tween my father & i*

iii.

this wound my daddy survive. i dig in th bloodmess ova & ova & call
it a poem. my daddy got a heifer fo' a daughter & love me
like a wound— awful. i airs his shit into a cold metal lattice
every thursday. kill his ego so quick, these fast lips itchin fo' a bruise. he dun
learned to withhold. i refuse to play wife inna home wit no heat
& now he leave me to ruin instead uh ballin his fists. aint that growths otha name?
eldest born of th red mud, miridional & audacious, I'm my father's daughter—
beveled by th third zone of his rage and th good, prodigious wild

i.

of course I wanted him to love me as if i was a boy-child. of course i wanted to earn
a man's birthright: respect by some otha name, th retiring of his fists against my side
i got none of these. I am only a girl who knew her mouth cud be a small fist upside
her daddy neck & if that wuz all the power I had, i shole wan't finna discard
it inna name of principle. myself I wuz sittin tall when men walked my way—expensive
and feral. if every man was a father, then i became the ruin of patralineage, the death
of my daddy by my hands, my thighs, my defiance. I wish i cud tell u the end was beautiful

filé

our blood thickens
in the porous swell

of august. this is the kind of summer we tend
to with impatience. the kind of summer we tend

to blame our father's absence on.
the honeysuckle rots violently in noon

soured sweat. the children beg for a couple
pennies & their innocence back. a desperate

exhaustion snags its tooth on the hem
of your mother's skirt. drags her damn

near off the steps. heat swelling into
your father's worst temper. his best

sunday mood, invading the corners
of any holy. up the block, thunder

chews on the bone of a clear day. it is always this kind
welt summer. always fire, bellowing from the estuary,

a barrel's mouth. this same kindred, same thick red
lust, same throttled burgundy. in a neighborhood

you are beloved. in a district, you are impending.
in a basement, your lover plays that one joint, allows

you a toke of amnesia. glides her hand up your thigh
begs you to dance. begs you to differ from the dead.

you oblige. you hide your pleasure, 'less someone run off
with it. you sweat like you running from something.

this damn heat. no one welcomes
the humid vice. 'cept these elders. the dogs.

police.

things that have seen worse.
been it, even.

egungun

if there is such a place/ where the dead walk/ & there is no/ mourning/ i am sure you are/ there/
brother/i am sure you are eating/ pork rind & dancing / windmills round/ the niggas we/ first
met in/ grandmothers good book/ wildthing/ i bet they call you/ i bet you cant hear/ them/
over the tender/ sound of a djembe flirting with your hips/ even there/ where the time dont
stop/i am sure you/ run late to everything/ i am sure nobody minds/ when you flash them/ that
sun swallowed mouth/ that unhinged glow/ brother/ i bet you/ if there is such a thing as God/
maker of the most trill dance floor/ he who rules/ the truest indigos/ Elohim/ who calls the
water/ into/ puddle/ into/ flood/ into /these tears carving my face/ i know/ you've renamed him/
my nigga/ have called to him/ *aye, OG!*/ down a long hallway/ full/ i am sure he answers with
a smile/ each time/ your voice swallows him/ in mischief/ in praise/ i imagine your shoulder
wet/ in the twilight of/ this third space/ this not hell, not earth/ this heaven by another name/
his head resting gently there/ his body the tremble/ of a wailing/ now subsided/ & you brother/
you a crooner/ & been one always/ you sing him your favorite/ *songs in the key of life*/ you let
him unfasten his whole self/ before he go back/ to being our god/ & the magic of it is/ you aint
no angel/ you aint   / you just you/ out there being light/ once/ when you knew you were
dying/ you told me to/ rest my head on your chest & listen/ I know it's silly/ to call the heart
a drum/ considering/ but damn/ if it wasn't music/ brother/ what was it?

wayward experiments

i. there is somewhere, a heaven just for
Black gxrls
& wherever it lives, the graves are empty there, soft
with
dew and satisfied by bodies
of laughter.
there, oceans return to their shores
with whole
clusters of us, or we ship
our mothers
love letters in the salt we gather at the feet
of magnolia trees,
empty the blessed sun
into our thighs and drink.
we choose this heaven:
one that doesn't quiet our other selves
we say *a-me, a-me, a-me* and mean
asé, axi, ache.
we pray to a god that wants no sacrifice
only asks that we sound out our names
only asks us to stay a while
& if we ever leave, keep the door open
for a few more gxrls

ii. say it's the end of days & all the world has left is us
Black gxrls running our hands over the wheat making
batteries from honey and mud say you've moved
on and your legacies will be written with *them* hands right there
say we will shrivel you or shine you say that fear is warranted now lock the doors
when you come down our block but you can't—you dead
say we stir our soups with your sun glint bones say your precious lawns we overrun
with lavender say honeysuckle say we burn your homes to make our frolic fields
a little wider say we masturbate in your churches say we bastardize
your holy say we gut god and gully our joy in his carcass
in new glory we ain't gotta explain how apples sound between two molars
in June or what it mean to be proven innocent say new heaven is full of innocence full
of guilt-free gxrls free of juries or taxes or tyrants say it is the end of days and all the world has
left is us standing 'neath a green sun with a clean pair of air force ones say it is the end
of days and we wake to find the trees uproot and the oceans sweet say we start new heaven
with sage and a wild song: janelle monae the sound of carpenters bees a thousand pulsating
oyster knives we will do the new world a favor and tell the truth maybe you were once
good but you left without making amends. maybe once you believed
in our freedom but then decided liberation was a myth we peer down from our new
glorious paradise to the place you landed we send the cores of our apples as gifts blemish your
mouth with our old sugar *our old sugar old sugar old sugar old sugar*

this poem is a hex, tread light

*a note: tear out & place with your r*pist's name in a jar of cayenne,*
redbrick dust, wasps, dog shit. Bury in a cemetery.
throw pennies at the intersections on your way home.

this poem untethers whatever flaccid ego you have
left, from its home beneath your gut
this poem an account to wound your pride,
to lace your woe with the waste of that night,
may you be ever-struck by fire or fear of being found out

/ / /

you are mid-smile in a bar
among old friends
a cold beer between your thumb
& that villainous forefinger

something about the weather
sliding out your littered teeth
a friend says yeah, *its gon rain* & then perhaps
well, have you done what she said you did

a clock crashes to the floor
& i could say *time's up*, but it's all too easy,
the shift. what little there is left to break
into a million strands of my hair.
gotcha.

hunted by my testimony
haunted by the ***no*** i left in your lap
be ye now withered into a void
and ever-removed from delight's door
you know no peace.
you exit the bar and leak my grief

in the periphery, i am grinning
as you stumble home. i wish you petrified
every shadow beneath a street lamp my dim skeleton.
quincy, you are a ruined man and my body has healed

/ / /

like a parasite, i make my own juice from your bones
i enjoy the simple humor of gluttony
outside your window, a wino sings My name
gotcha.

i am softening in the face of my suffering
i am softening in the face of my suffering
i am softening in the face of my suffering.
asé. asé. asé.

your wife bears witness.
asks if you've raped *anyone else, lately.*
gotcha.

of course, i got got, first.
So long ago, i know you've forgotten
the summer i chose your brother
and as punishment, you chose me, quincy
no matter my own convictions.
forced my mouth to do that ugly magic

at the altar i engulfed fire
created arithmetic for new flesh
so i wouldn't lose

myself in the dagger of my grief.
i am whole now, and
usher in nothing but hot powder at your feet
you have earned a lifetime of thorn, of dismaterial love.
you have earned seven years of my scent cloying your tongue,
                                        , papercuts in your soft flesh
        my nails against your firstborn's neck
        a fleeting and terrible death. asé.

psalm in which i demand a new name for my kin

after Danez Smith

Brandi
Nautica
Ember
Tiff
Kadazia
ChE
Simoine
Denisha
Rain
Chari
Sentura
Kiki
Tianna
Victoria
Nabila
Imani

I swear on my mother's laugh, *friend* don't cut it.
you caught a bitch in her early nude, paper
thin psalms sharpened into blades on her mother's
lawn, what a mess and you loved her fiercely.
not *sister*, but *salvation of noise*. your broke ass
hands the arithmetic of Five Points
the library dust in your bones perhaps a way to sing
my favorite poem, over a cliff. *my dark*
bloody muse, my nigga. I love you
in the worst way. I mouth pomegranate
in gummy bliss & the kernels fall like manna
into your lap. I milk honeysuckle and your belly
swells with child, *my love* you are *mine*.
how do I say it plain? your youngest born is an other
me, your blood beneath his skin and my teeth in his mouth.
you spit and I blush into chlorine at Mozley Park.
not *homegxrl* but *my bluest magic*, the wicked
sunday morning song I scythe
from my mother's hair like hot
oil. when we feast in your kitchen
we commune, bitch you *my whole lyric*.
ain't I said it enough, that you love
like an orange? I pull you from the vine and weep
at how many times you have halved in my
palm and not slipped away. not *bitch* but *bitch, you tender*
me. you give me better language for my
broken. whats the word? *my dawg*, you gift me the gutter
squad as in *I'll never pretend to fix my love*
into a hymn. a rope of braid at my navel, you *the whole soup*
you *the roux of me, my solemn chew, my nigga*
you *the gristle*, I love you the bone splinter
I love you the gum ache, I love you the jigsaw sweat
the deep sigh, the belly slick, the muscled

Kelsey
'Nez
Jada
Sophia
Brandilyn
Isis

sprint from sun to dusk, you *the star*
I follow to rid myself the Mason Dixon
I line you up over my father's toilet
when I bleed you gather my family to pray
when I pray you beckon my mother's god
to listen, *my god, my best friend* I love you,
I love you and am alive to witness you be this great iteration
this majestic selfishness. my mama say
she got 12 kids and birthed only three
& the world was formed in how many days?
I wish that same holy multiplication upon our children
our thick-headed young, a legion of fool ass saints
linked at the hip of their glory. tethered just like this here, long after we dead.

in the event i become some unrecognizable beast

reader, it is so simple:
i am a tender bird
parading as this vulture.

i love things unto their very bone
& yet have always
held grief a fragile vein
or deprived myself its honey.

i misplace what simple sanities i meant to keep
precious: my composure, a bloodlet.
the teeth from my mouth also,

left to accordion the homes we flee like fugitives
evictions among the weathered estate
of our arms & all i manage
to carry into each line is a mason
jar of old bones, a cicada, an aged bruise.

the thing is; grief
is relative. i wake to the limp
memory of missing kindred each day
& what do you know about endurance?
            by noon each day, i'm dancing to the hook
            of my brother's last song, a wild
flocking. i raise my hands & cut the tumor
from between his hips. the moon rises. there, we rest
our bodies into the egun. We sliver beneath it. can you name them?
this conjuring morbid, yes. and also,

necessary. what else can a forager do? reader, you've stolen my
meat, the marrow and tendon. i shape myself a body worthy
of your fear. i give myself hands, and build myself a mirror.
i give myself a jaw then splinter it. i prepare myself into a feast.

i bring ritual in the creole of angels—
my mother's tongue. i bring with me, salt and what i've done
with tobacco. am i not an altar? have we not emerged on the other side,
full? you are welcome. and i am well.

i am only a flutter thing.
from my beak   *i pull three nylon sutures.*
i've eaten from my own soft & stayed
                                                            Alive.

MORE NOTES

gxrl gospel i takes its name from the canonical Black Feminist anthology *Some of Us Are Brave*, coedited by Akasha Gloria Hull, Patricia Bell-Scott, and Barbara Smith. It is an ekphrastic poem inspired by Camonghne Felix's *Build Yourself a Boat*. Rekia Boyd and Muhlaysia Booker, both referenced in the work, are two Black women killed as a result of structural racism, misogynoir, and violence.

war strategies for every hood was written for Dajerria Becton, a fifteen-year-old who was brutalized by a McKinney, Texas, police officer who swung the girl-child down to the ground by her braid extensions.

pantoum for aiyanna and not a single hashtag is written in honor of Aiyanna Stanley-Jones, a seven-year-old girl who was shot by police while sleeping in her home after their stun grenade lit her blanket on fire. The murder was captured by A&E's *The First 48*. The home they meant to enter was on the floor directly above where Aiyanna had been sleeping.

gxrl gospel ii takes after both poet Morgan Parker's "I Feel Most Colored When I Am Thrown Against A Sharp White Background: An Elegy" and conceptual artist Glen Ligon's *i feel most colored* (which Parker's poem is also after). Both are inspired by Zora Neale Hurston's essay, "How It Feels to Be Colored Me."

portrait of rage with caution tape & bullhorns is written exclusively with words uttered by Erica Garner, daughter of Eric Garner who was killed by police in 2014, in speeches, interviews, and personal conversations. After her father's death, Erica became a leader in movements against police brutality, and fought for her father's killers to face proper trial until her death in 2017. State violence killed both Eric Garner and his daughter.

i, too, sing america takes its name from the Langston Hughes poem, and has a tone stylized similarly to that of Destiny Birdsong's poem of the same name.

gxrl gospel iii manipulates phrases found in Lucille Clifton's "won't you celebrate with me," Maya Angelou's "Caged Bird," and the gospel song "His Eye Is on the Sparrow."

~~*no name in the street*~~ borrows its name from James Baldwin's fourth nonfiction book, which addressed different figures and events concerning State-sanctioned violence and State-persecution of 1960s civil rights leaders.

father-son & holy pulls shape, language, and tone from Audre Lorde's poem "Father Son and Holy Ghost."

some of the men we love are terrorists gets its name from the last line of the poem "Romance Is Intrigue" by Essex Hemphill.

The last words on each line of the sestina *a poem of failures*, together make up the primary refrain found in Langston Hughes's poem "Mother to Son."

The title poem *gumbo ya ya* pulls an excerpt from a *New York Times* piece covering the death of Atatiana Jefferson. Jefferson was killed by a police officer while babysitting her nephew, after a neighbor called in for a wellness check to her home.

transhistorical & i observe the sabbath like a ill verse was written while listening exclusively to Noname's feature on Finish Line/Drown, a song on Chance the Rapper's freshman album, *Coloring Book*. The poem and her verse share vocabulary.

like a freedom too strange to be conquered got its name from a speech by Kim Katrin and then-husband Tiq Milan where, in describing the fugitive possibilities of queerness, she pulls a quote from poet Brandon Wint: "Not 'queer' like 'gay.' 'Queer' like escaping definition. 'Queer' like some sort of fluidity and limitlessness at once. 'Queer' like a freedom too strange to be conquered . . . "

I think it is important, always, to name our ancestors. My egun made a way for me, and just as I have egun, so too does *Gumbo Ya Ya*. This book wouldn't exist without the hard work and courage and articulation I found in the pages of Madame Louisa Teish's *Jumbalaya*, the mud from which this book conjured itself into being. Camonghe Felix's *Build Yourself a Boat*, Danez Smith's *Insert [Boy]*, Nabila Lovelace's *Sons of Achilles*, and god damn T'ai Freedom Ford's *How to Get Over*, each hallowed out places to locate and contextualize my own x. And, Xandria Phillips's *Hull*, which I was too scared to read until this book was done, turned out to be a North Star for us anyway.

These texts are foundational and worthy of your support.

ACKNOWLEDGMENTS

Reader, I been waitin so long for this book to reach you. For those who held on beside me, fingers crossed, thank you. I can hardly believe we made it! We share these words now, co-owners and partners in rabble.

Endless gratitude to the editors of these journals for their early faith in many of the poems contained in this book: *Ploughshares*, *The Adroit Journal*, *BOAAT*, *Blue Mesa Review*, *Southeast Review*, *Sycamore Review*, *Vinyl*, *SELFISH*, *Scalawag*, *Barrelhouse*, *TriQuarterly*, *Michigan Quarterly Review*, *Split Lip Magazine*, *Los Angeles Review*, *Florida Review*, *Poem-a-Day*, *The Shallow Ends*, *Palette Poetry*, *The Rumpus*, and the Center for Women Writers.

Grace to former publishers for making it so that this work joins the league of queer kids kicked out they first home and then saved by chosen family. Asé to the kiln and the other side. Asé to choosing.

So much deep joy and thanks to the generous support from William and Sue and the entire Lambda Literary organization, Tin House (though I ain't made it over there just yet), VONA, The Watering Hole, Pink Door, Kopkind Colony, and Winter Tangerine for offering me solace and space to toil with this work, deepen it, sharpen it, and make it true.

Thank you Cave Canem and the incomparable Douglas Kearney for choosing *Gumbo Ya Ya*. I am grateful to an absolutely silly degree. Thank you, too, to the entire University of Pittsburgh Press team. Chloe, Alex, Kelly, John, and everyone else who had a hand in truly the most painless and beautiful publication process ever. Bless each those hands!

Thank you Tschalalaba Self, for allowing us to use your breathless work for the cover. You don't know how much it meant. Bless your hands too!

Singing high praise for my agent, Janet Silva, who helped me through the literary mountains and valleys long before I ever signed a dotted line.

I would be nowhere without the love and support of my family, particularly my mother Renee Hutcherson Lucier. Mommy, I love you deeper and wider than any metaphor could ever touch! Thank you for letting me trace my own way, a young and foolish cartographer. Thank you for trusting my voice when I couldn't. Thank you for putting your kids on your back while you crossed that river. You the whole poem.

To my father, Vincent Lucier, you gifted me the whole sum of my Blackness and also Langston and the real world while I was still too young. Thank you. It served me well. To my siblings Nautica, Luke and Bobby, and the sister-cousins and brother-cousins, I love you. Rest well, Sarah, James, and Josiah. MJ, I'm grateful to be one of yours. To the Weesum Family and the Gumbo-folk, the Mitchells and Walker-Zacharys, the Samuels, the Babineauxs, the Texas, Connecticut, and California cousins, and Teece and the extended Wallace family: I carry you, too.

Rest in Ultimate Power, Leonardo Lucier, Jr. Missing you every day. It ain't music like we planned, but I hope you're proud.

To homie-teachers and kindred ones, you who kept me true to my voice, grounded in spirit, rigorous and with my chin up: Nabila, Imani Davis, Jada, Kendra, Sarah Panlubuton Barnes, Victoria (Cousin!), KiKi, Faylita, Pages, Mariah, I love y'all BIG! Additional gratitude and all its vulnerable, silly delight to writers whose support helped me keep the faith: Phillip B Williams, Julian, Luther, Safiya Sinclair, Alison, Bettina Judd, Regina Bradley, Raquel, Camonghne, Joy Priest, Morgan Parker, Nancy Huang, Tina, Rasha, Cortney, Hanif, Nate, Maya Marshall, Gabriel, Willie, Sadia, Nicholas, Kenzie Allen, and everyone who gathered on the orange couch in Oakland or the green couch in Alabama. Thank you for being in praxis with me.

I simply must give high honor to the day ones, the original crews.

> Simoine, Chari, Isis, Sophia, Kell, Brandilyn, my hometown heroes. Y'all have grown and flexed with me over the years, y'all suffer my stubbornness. Wherever life takes us, you will always be the we of me.

Humbled and sitting with love for Bronte, Natalie, Janetta, Nadia May, Itsel, Adam, and the whole Atlanta Word Works OG squad (Kali! Saicryd!). Slam was my first home. Thank you for trudging through my angry years. Loving on you wherever you are. A-Dub for life.

Tianna and Che, I take satisfaction knowing our ancestors conspired so we could walk this life together. I would have given up without you. Love you deeper than a colonizer's tongue allows.

Unending tenderness for Da'Shaun, Eva, Simi, Hunter, Asia, Eshe, Avry, Carter, Tif, Crystal, Tea, Brittany Packenyett Cunningham, and my entire organizing family, Atlanta and beyond. Praise that we are fugitive. May these words feel like a balm against all we've lost and survived.

Zoë, it's you and me in this life and god, what a gift. Thank you for your belief and your love. I won't spoil my vows in this book (lol). Just know.

The mentors I've had across the years deserve their roses, now and always. Danez, thank you. You've trudged along with this book since its inception. You held me. There'd be no *Gumbo Ya Ya* without you. Whew. Thank you Ryka Aoiki, my sister-mother, for demanding everything but my silence. Thank you Dr. Bettina Love, for clocking me when I was just a loud ass gxrl with promise. Blessings to Zinta and the original Angel, Wendy. Thank you Patricia Smith, for knowing. Thank you L Lamar Wilson, Rachel McKibbens, Camille Dungy, my thesis advisor, Kwoya Maples, Tyehimba Jess, Nicole Sealey (minus them lions in Kenya), and the many other folks who have guided my steps over the years.

Ooo, all my niggas. You just don’t know how much I love you.

Now take these words and go do some good with em.